A Road Map for World Peace

By

Rev. James D. Kimmel

This book is a work of non-fiction. Names and places have been changed to protect the privacy of all individuals. The events and situations are true.

ISBN: 1-4140-1714-6 (e-book)
ISBN: 1-4140-1715-4 (Paperback)

This book is printed on acid free paper.

1stBooks - rev. 12/20/03

I. Introduction

About one hundred years ago, in 1905, Dr. Albert Einstein published a report on the mass equivalence equation, $E = mc^2$. At the same time, Dr. E. N. Transeau led the way in the creation of the Ecological Society of America. The mass-equivalence equation provided insight and understanding relative to the creation of the atomic bomb and the birth of the Atomic Age. My father-to-be was just ten years old at this time; Hawai'i had recently been overthrown and was occupied by the U. S. government. The citizens of the Kingdom of Hawai'i had been made American citizens by the U. S. government. John D. Rockefeller and his friends were then deeply involved in activities designed to get them power and control over the future Central Bank of America-to-be, the United States Federal Reserve System.

Shortly after America declared war in 1941, it was rumored that Hitler was sponsoring research on a new kind of weapon, an atomic bomb. The fear of Hitler getting such an incredible war club led then President Roosevelt to inquire of Dr. Einstein as to the reality of such a potential weapon, and he was assured that it was a real possibility. With Dr. Einstein's "endorsement," President Roosevelt decided that the United States government would have to create such a bomb before

1

Hitler's supposed efforts were successful. The program to do the research and all other things necessary to build and test an atomic bomb was known as the Manhattan Project and was launched in great secrecy under the watchful care of General Lesley R. Groves.

On March 1, 1954, the United States government detonated a 15-megaton thermonuclear bomb at Bikini Atoll in the Marshall Islands. The fallout grossly contaminated the pristine environment of Rongelap Atoll and the human beings living in this extraordinary ecosystem. The world was informed that a Japanese fishing boat, the Lucky Dragon, with its crew and load of tuna were seriously contaminated with radioactive fallout from the Bravo Shot at Bikini.

At this time, I was 19 years old and a sophomore at The Ohio State University in Columbus, Ohio. I had entered Ohio State in the fall of 1953 as a means of continuing my competitive swimming career in college. I had no real idea of what I wanted to major in and had started out in their pre-veterinary medicine program. During this period, I had an opportunity to schedule an elective class along with my required schedule. Not knowing what to take, I consulted with my swimming team buddies, and one of them suggested signing up for general botany. "Don't laugh bra," they said, "The study of plants is something you'll really like, and it's an easy A or B."

Just as I was beginning my study of plants, Dr. Transeau was retiring as the Chairman Emeritus of the Department of Botany and Plant Pathology at Ohio State. Before leaving, he was approached by Congressional staffers seeking his knowledge and insight relative to the ecological effects of nuclear and thermonuclear weapons testing on the environment. He suggested that the man they needed to talk to for the questions they needed answers to was a plant ecologist named Dr. John N. Wolfe, my adviser.

Dr. Wolfe was soon called to testify before a U. S. Congressional Committee seeking knowledge about the biological effects of radiation. They were startled by his response to one of their questions about the ecological effects of radioactivity when he told them they were 20 years late in asking the question. Natural levels of background radioactivity, as an ecological factor in the evolution of life on earth, had been changed on a global level, and there was no before to compare the after to. Fallout from the northern hemisphere was already being found in the icy snows of Antarctica, proving that there was circulation and mixing of air masses that crossed back and forth over the equator into the northern and southern hemispheres.

During Christmas vacation in 1954, I went to Fort Lauderdale, Florida, to work out with other members of the swimming team getting ready for the season coming up during winter quarter. Skin diving was just getting started as a water sport, and I was having a ball discovering the world under the waters of the Florida Keys where I discovered *Lobster heaven* around the bottoms of the pillars of concrete holding up the bridges between the Keys.

Shortly after getting back to Ohio State for the winter quarter and the swimming season, I told my Hawaiian buddy on the swim team, Dick Cleveland, about all the lobsters I saw under the bridges of the Florida Keys. We abruptly decided to drop out of school and head for the Florida Keys to dive up lobsters. It was a very successful venture, and we celebrated by spending two weeks in Cuba during Mardi Gras since it was only $25 for a round-trip ticket from Key West to Havana at the time.

Returning to Ohio State for the spring quarter of 1955 found me taking more botany courses and deciding to change my major from pre-vet medicine to botany. I had found that the study of plants was thoroughly captivating and most enjoyable. The more I studied plants, the more I learned about myself since I had discovered that animals had evolved from plants and were 100% dependent on plants for their very existence! I was learning that the study of plants was the most basic life science I could find to begin figuring out how life started on earth.

Philosophically, I was a twenty-year-old atheist at the time. The church I had been exposed to as a child by my mother had scared me out of believing in God by the time I was a teenager. The fear of hell, fire, and brimstone wasn't good enough to scare me into believing. The fear of God, the last days, the second-coming of Jesus, the terrible times of tribulation, and the *Anti-Christ* at hand were all too scary to believe. The answers to all of my questions at Sunday school seldom seemed to "ring my truth bell." It took a lot of courage to come to the conclusion that my mother, my Sunday school teachers, and the preacher at church were all wrong somehow, and it was on me to figure out what the truth was. One thing was for sure; I was not willing to accept a religion which was inconsistent with facts and out of harmony with my highest conceptions of truth, beauty, and goodness.

I used to drive my parents and teachers crazy trying to get answers to questions that kept rising up in my mind. I was terribly curious, and my parents' family farm was teeming with all kinds of thought-stimulating, environmentally related components. We lived on a family dairy farm in the Deciduous Forest region of North America located in northeastern Ohio. There were four very distinct seasons of the year, and the ice froze over the three lakes nestled in the midst of the Mixed Mesophytic type of forest natural to the area. But where did all those huge boulders come from scattered around the lakes and around about the cleared areas that we farmed? Where did everything I was discovering in my home environment come from? What was life all about, and where did the frogs and turtles go in the wintertime when the lakes were all frozen over?

My mom and dad always did their best to answer all of my questions, but I soon learned that they didn't really know either; so I'd ask someone else, like the hired man or my Sunday school teacher. If their answers didn't ring my truth bell, I would just keep on asking anyone I thought might know. What was the cause of day and night, summer and winter, spring and fall? What did it all mean? I think my faith in the church was finally shattered when I discovered the truth about what really happens to the turtles and fish and frogs in the wintertime when it is so terribly cold and frozen over as I well knew from growing up there.

My Sunday school teacher told me not to worry about such things because God took them up to heaven to be with Him in the wintertime! I was beginning to learn that most people didn't seem to know the answers to all the questions that wouldn't go away until I learned the truth about whatever the question related to.

One of the things I loved to do as a kid was to roam around my dad's farm, especially the lakes and forest parts catching frogs, snakes, turtles, fish, birds, or whatever. The first time I heard anyone talking about Indian Summers came, and it was an early winter. Things got cold; the ice started skimming over the lakes, and there was an early snow on the ground. The frogs and turtles had long since disappeared from the scene, having left for heaven during the night when I couldn't see them go.

Then things started getting warm again. The snow melted, the ice on the lakes disappeared, and then one day, imagine my astonishment to see some turtles sticking their heads out of the water and others sunning themselves on the logs and rocks in the water along the shore. I was all excited, sneaking up as close as I could get to the nearest of them, and then, dashing forward to try and catch one or two of them. Anyhow, I overshot my mark and ended up falling forward in the very cold water with my hands penetrating the muddy bottom, stopping only when I hit what I thought was a rock. But then the *rock* moved, and I realized it was a turtle. What was a turtle doing deep down in this mud when he was supposed to be in heaven with God? This was my first reaction. Then I started feeling around in the muck, and, lo and behold, I began finding other turtles and, what's this? A big bullfrog, all cooled down and groggy with the cold, but definitely not in heaven.

Disillusionment was sweet, but traumatic. I had discovered more facts and truths about life on my own as I learned, increasingly, that I could not depend on everyone else to know the answers to life's persistent questions that life raised

7

in my mind. By the time I was finished with high school, I was ripe and ready for college and whatever I was going to discover on a higher level.

Choosing Ohio State was a natural. They had many of the best swimmers in the world on their team, and I had met all of them during my high school career as a state scholastic swimming champion on a state champion high school team at Canton McKinley High School. The state finals were always held in Columbus, the capitol, at the Ohio State Natatorium, and I was a welcomed newcomer to the scene in the fall of 1953.

I was still looking for a place to find answers to some of my biggest questions, like what is life, and how did it get started on earth, and where do we all come from? So far at Ohio State, I had concluded that life probably got started in the oceans of the past, so, in the fall of 1956, I decided to check out the University of Hawai'i, situated right in the middle of the North Pacific Ocean! Perhaps I could find what I was looking for on the frontiers of marine biology!

Failing that, I proposed to the wonderful woman I had found and wanted to marry and have children with. Cordelia Elizabeth Wysard was the daughter of Martha Hartwell and Paul Wysard. At this time, Hawai'i was a territory of the United States. I knew absolutely nothing of the history of Hawai'i, nor how things had come to be the way they are in Hawai'i today. I had no idea how significant all this was until the winter of 1973 when I read *Hawaii's Story* by Hawaii's Queen, Liliuokalani.

In reading this book, *Hawaii's Story* by Hawaii's Queen, I discovered that my children, James, Paul, and Kimberly, through their mother, Cordelia, were the great-great grandchildren of A. S. Hartwell, Attorney General to the Queen and the lawyer who purportedly drew up the papers of abdication the Queen was forced to sign under threat of bloodshed.

I had found a righteous cause worthy of devoting my energies toward the making right of a great wrong that had been committed by the United States government—the illegal overthrow and occupation of the Kingdom of Hawai'i by the U. S. government and the theft of some 4 million acres of the National and Crown Lands! The tragedy of the Americanization of Hawai'i is nothing less than a species of treason and genocide that would exterminate the Hawaiian identity and relinquish all rightful claims of their inherent sovereignty.

Not long after our marriage, my wife and I returned to Columbus, Ohio, so I could resume my studies in the department of botany. Plant ecology was a whole new discovery that seemed to be the most basic of all the courses I had taken so far. At this time, Dr. Gareth Gilbert was teaching plant ecology for Dr. Wolfe who was on leave consulting with the Atomic Energy Commission in Washington, D. C. I loved studying plant ecology. At last I was getting answers to all the questions raised as a kid on my fathers farm, most of them anyhow. I looked forward to finally meeting the great Dr. Wolfe when he returned from Washington and thus began a great friendship with the man who contributed most to my higher education.

Talking story with Dr. Wolfe was probably my most favorite activity in undergraduate and graduate school. We'd go out to Cenci's Bar and Grill for a beer or two and have a good time philosophizing and playing *thought-ball*. After one of his many trips to Washington, he informed me that there was no codified bibliography on the subject of the biological or ecological effects of radiation or atomic fallout on the environment. As we talked things over, he suggested I might want to get some graduate credit for a special problems graduate course. This would involve my going to the library to begin the research necessary to compile the bibliography so badly needed. I thought this was a great opportunity, so I naturally went for it.

To get a handle on the ecological effects of nuclear weapons testing was essential to any continuation of the major nuclear testing programs underway. I'll never forget the day I was going through all the back issues of *Nuclear Science Abstracts* when I came across the report, complete with many graphic pictures of men, women, and children of the horrendous consequences of the testing of a 15-megaton thermonuclear bomb at Bikini Atoll, involving the people of Rongelap and Utirik atolls.

The big question for the American politicians was how far could they go using nuclear and thermonuclear weapons? They needed to know about the personal and ecological effects of using weapons of the greatest possible mass destruction, and here was an opportunity to maximize insight and understanding to the problem. A micro-ecosystem isolated some 5,000 miles from the nearest continental land mass, which included land and ocean plants and animals in all their relationships with the people of Rongelap Atoll. The entire continuum of the personality-ecosystem of Rongelap Atoll was typical of what one might find after an all-out nuclear war. Rongelap has been adversely affected to this day, to say nothing of Eniwetok, Bikini, and Utirik.

If the population had not been evacuated after two days of whole body internal and external exposure to the BRAVO fallout, they all would have died. As it was, there was much radiation sickness and many skin ulcerations. Abortions and still-births were numerous and are still continuing. If the people had been living at the northern end of the atoll, such as on Kabelle Island, they all would have been killed—murdered, from overexposure to radiation in less than a day. Was this so-called accident necessary, or did the U. S. government use these people as guinea pigs when they didn't have to? I know this for sure: If they could evacuate them after the explosion, they could have evacuated them before the explosion!

After I reported on my findings to Dr. Wolfe, we had several long talks during which I told him I would love to go to Rongelap Atoll to do research for a thesis and otherwise fulfill the requirements for receiving the degree, Master of Science. I thought this would be a perfect place to observe and study the ecological effects of nuclear weapons testing, and it was. The frontiers of ecology and nuclear weapons testing had merged, and soon I found myself on the leading edge with a team of scientists from the University of Washington's Laboratory of Radiation Biology heading for the Eniwetok Proving Grounds enroute to Rongelap Atoll in the summer of 1958.

Not long after receiving the degree master of science in the spring of 1960, I joined forces with a fellow ecologist from Ohio State, Dr. Janice Beatley, doing basic research at the Nevada test site for UCLA's Laboratory of Nuclear Medicine and Radiation Biology. This was a great opportunity to compare consequences of nuclear testing in the continental testing areas of Nevada with those in the central Pacific Ocean. The people and lands downwind of the nuclear tests all took gas. Many Americans residing in Nevada, Utah, California, and Arizona during the days of atmospheric testing have gone through the equivalent of a limited nuclear war. And as expected from what we found at Rongelap, the "downwinders" were found to have a plethora of thyroid problems following the intake of radioactive iodine, which concentrates in the thyroid and salivary glands.

II. From the Frying Pan into the Fire

After ten years on this frontier, I had had enough. I had to get out of working for the United States government. After turning down a three-year fellowship for a Ph.D. in biophysics and medical physics at Berkeley, I found myself teaching human biology and algebra at Novato High School in Marin County, California, just across the Golden Gate bridge from San Francisco. It was the summer of 1967, the *Summer of Love*, and it was a mind-blowing experience compared to where I had been the last ten years "behind closed doors." Marijuana and LSD were everywhere it seemed, and I knew nothing about anything except alcohol and tobacco when it came to drugs.

By the end of the school term at Christmas vacation time, my students had my back up against the wall on the subject of marijuana. They told me over and over that if I really wanted to know the truth about pot, I would have to try some—I would have to smoke it! I knew all about doing research with plants, and Doc Wolfe had always taught that the final test of any laboratory work was in the field under natural conditions. So I tried pot over Christmas vacation and then wondered why everyone didn't smoke it! I thought it was great! And there was *no hangover* like with too much beer or booze!

14

It took the better part of the first year to assess the environmental situation in which I found myself. The students were there because they were forced to be there, and they didn't care about learning the subject matter. After talking things over with my anthropology students during an archeological dig in the summer of 1968, I decided to take a new approach to my responsibility as a teacher and start a whole new way of teaching in the fall. I figured that if I could find some way to share the essence of everything I knew to be factual and true with my students, we'd all be at the same level of understanding and sense in common, i.e., common sense.

In the fall of 1968, my assignment at Novato High School included teaching classes in human biology, earth science, and physics, and being coach of the swimming and water polo teams. I told all my students in all my classes that things were going to be different that year. There would be no text, no homework, and no need to worry about grades because everyone was going to get an A. I didn't want them to feel any pressure or worry about grades. It was all about questions and answers.

I started off the session with each of my classes by asking: "Is everybody here?"

And finally someone said: "Yeah, we're all here." And I asked: "Which is where?" And momentarily someone said: "Room 13." And I asked: "Which is where?" And someone said:

"Novato High School." So I asked: "Which is where? And the answer was Novato, California. I then asked: "Which is where? And someone said; "The United States." And I asked: Which is where? I then heard: "North America." So I asked: "Which is where? "The planet earth," came the answer. Then I asked: "Which is where? And someone said: "The Solar System." And I asked: "Which is where?" And a voice said: "The Milky Way galaxy." And I asked: "Which is where?' And someone answered: "The universe." So I asked: "Which is where? Several voices said: "It's everywhere." And I asked: "Is it infinite?" And everyone finally agreed: "Yes, we are all here in what appears to be an infinite universe."

That being the natural end of that line of questioning, the inquiry continued by my asking: "Now that we know where *here* is, what is the universe made of?"

I started writing down the words they gave me on the blackboard and continued on until words completely covered the blackboard. Then, when the blackboard was full of words that described what they knew the universe consisted of, I asked: "What are the things that make up the universe made of?" What we found was that most of the words listed symbolized something physical, such as water, air, trees, soil, rocks, autos, cows, horses, stars, electricity, etc., etc., etc.

Some of the remaining words symbolized various intellectual realities of the mind, such as time and space, ideas, thoughts, preexistent potentials, and language. Others symbolized spiritual reality, such as truth, beauty, goodness, love, fairness, mercy, forgiveness, and other values. Finally, words like God, Jesus, personality, free will, morals, ethics, and soul were included. So when we finally sorted and sifted all of the words on the blackboard, we had delineated four infinite continua in four major dimensions—matter, mind, spirit (things, meanings, and values), and personality—physical reality, mindal reality, spiritual reality, and personality reality.

At this juncture, I asked: "What are the things that make up the universe made of?" referring to all of those words on the blackboard that symbolized something physical. And no matter what word we examined, at base level, they were all different versions of the same thing—physical energy-matter made up of atoms—electrons, protons, neutrons, and subatomic particles.

Dr. Einstein said that if you took a straight line and extended it in equal and opposite directions from a point source, it would close on itself in infinity. I don't know why that is supposed to be true. But I had been teaching algebra, and the number line came to mind. You remember the number line? It looks something like this:

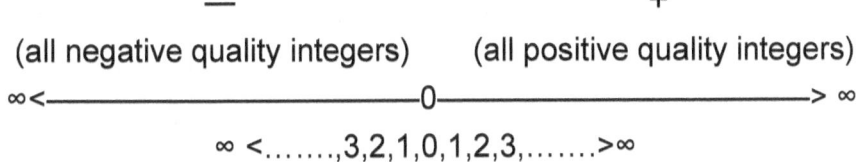

— +

(all negative quality integers) (all positive quality integers)

$\infty < \!\!-\!\!-\!\!-\!\!-\!\!-\!\!-\!\!-\!\!-\!\!0\!\!-\!\!-\!\!-\!\!-\!\!-\!\!-\!\!-\!\!-\!\!> \infty$

$\infty <.......,3,2,1,0,1,2,3,.......> \infty$

17

Now, if you take this simple number line and give it an "Einsteinian twist" extending it in equal and opposite directions from zero point to infinity, it would look something like the symbol for infinity, thusly:

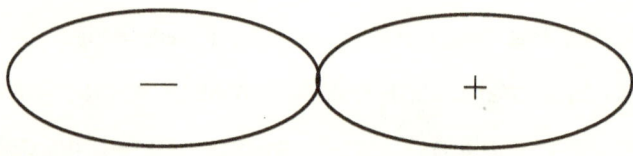

The point source, 0, is the point of origin. This represents the absolute as a source relativity, an absolute cause in contrast to a relative effect. It could also represent the geographic center of infinity. All of the positive quality integers in infinity constitute one infinite continuum, and all of the negative quality integers constitute another. Together, three infinite dimensions are delineated, two relative and one absolute which, in itself, is infinite, i.e., an absolute singularity, the source of the infinite continuum.

Now, as far as numbers and the number line are concerned, there are no numbers in infinity without or before someone to use them, say the first great mathematician, the source of numbers. Which came first, the mathematician or the numbers he uses? Personalities use numbers, and are antecedent to numbers in infinity. Numbers represent something while zero represents nothing because there can be no such actuality as nothing. One quantum unit of nothing would be something!

Everything and everybody has to have a source-cause. There is a cause for every effect. We are personal effects living in a universe of relative effects produced by various causes, which have their relative origins in the absolutes of infinity, as described by the number line. The Universe, being an infinite effect, implies there is an absolute and infinite cause for all of the major relativities in space, including space itself.

Of all the words put on the blackboard, some symbolized superphysical realities. There were those that symbolized intellectual, mindal realities, which were manifestations of mindal energy, and others that symbolized manifestations of living and spiritual realities symbolic of purposeful, spiritual energy. There were also those that symbolized realities of personality, including self-consciousness, free will choice, and morality. And to make it all real simple, the number line can be used to show the absolutes and the relativities of seven infinite continua in seven dimensions of universe reality.

A trip to the Lawrence Radiation Laboratory at Berkeley was an eye-opening experience for my students and me in the fall of 1968. We saw what happens when you slam an electron into a pool of protons at 98% of the velocity of the speed of light, 186,280 miles per second. A pool of liquid hydrogen is almost entirely protons. Each atom is a trifle over

1/100,000,000th of an inch in diameter while the electron weighs a little over 1/2,000th of the hydrogen atom. High-speed photography visualizes dramatically what happens to charged and uncharged particles in an electromagnetic field.

When the electron hits the proton, the integrity of the atom is shattered, and both the electron and the proton are broken into smaller, subatomic and subelectronic units or *quanta* of energy. Some were positively charged, some were negatively charged, and some were neutral in charge. As small as the components of atoms are, there are subatomic and subelectronic components that are even smaller as well. These include such entities as mesons, muons, pions, mesotrons, bosons, quarks, neutrinos, and the smallest of all physical energy units, the *ultimaton*. It is believed that 100 ultimatons make one electron while each ultimaton has a superphysical nucleus, one quantum unit of absolute gravity, which over-controls the entire continuum of the physical energy system.

So when I asked my students: "What are the things that make up the things that make up the physical universe made of?", we had a great discussion from all the insight gained from the radiation laboratory field trip. When we were finished, we had concluded that all of the physical energy-matter in the universe was made up of positive, negative, and neutrally charged particles at base level. Light, heat, electricity, magnetism, chemism, energy, and matter are all different versions of one basic thing—physical energy: $E = mc^2$! The infinite continuum shown by the number line can be used to demonstrate how all of the physical energy-matter in the universe is made up of a triunity of negative, neutral, and positive charged components at base level:

$$\infty(-) \longleftarrow\hspace{-0.5em}\text{---------------}\hspace{-0.5em})0(\hspace{-0.5em}\text{---------------}\hspace{-0.5em}\longrightarrow (+) \infty$$

     electrons   neutrons   protons

In our pursuit of knowledge, wisdom, and truth, we had discovered that, at base level, all of the material reality of the universe was made up of positive, neutral, or negatively charged quanta. Every atom of every element of every compound of anything anywhere in the universe was a different version of the same thing everything else is: physical energy-matter, physical light in some form and phase or another. Nuclear and thermonuclear explosions transmute and transform matter into pure energy. The light from the first atomic explosion, code named *TRINITY*, was described by Dr. J. Robert Oppenheimer as "brighter than ten thousand suns"!

In the physical energy universe, for every action there is an equal and opposite reaction, which is true and steadfast in its obedience to universal law. When it comes to a person or persons, there is not always an equal and opposite reaction because of the endowment of free will. When it comes to persons, because of the power and freedom to choose, you may or may not get back what you put out. Man can choose positive, negative, or neutral positions relative to any issue of conduct or matter of choice, and he can even return good for evil or evil for good.

The intellectual and spiritual energies that make up the dimensions of mindal and spiritual reality are likewise made up of the triunity of positive, neutral, and negative potentials and actuals. There are good ideas, evil ideas, and neutral ideas; there are positive, negative, and neutral experiences in life. We are talking about physical reality, intellectual (mindal) reality, and spiritual reality. Personal reality is volitional, but will power is not the energy of matter, mind, or spirit. Personality reality is moral or immoral at base level, as a matter of freewill choice. At base level, we are *will creatures*, moral or immoral, as a matter of choice.

There is a thin line between good and evil, joy and sorrow, truth and error, fact and fiction, and you always get just what you choose.

The four dimensions of personality reality, spiritual reality, mindal reality, and physical reality are all infinite in potential and actual phases as can all be shown by the simple and basic, but modified, number line.

Understanding everything in the universe is one thing that naturally raises another question: Where do the things that make up the things that make up the universe come from? Again, we can get a clue from the simple number line:

$$\begin{array}{ccc} - & 0 & + \end{array}$$

$$\infty <\!\!-\!\!-\!\!-\!\!-\!\!-\!\!-\!\!-\!\!-\!\!-\!\!-\!\!-\!\!0\!\!-\!\!-\!\!-\!\!-\!\!-\!\!-\!\!-\!\!-\!\!-\!\!-\!\!-> \infty$$

$$\infty <\ldots\ldots,3,2,1,0,1,2,3,\ldots\ldots> \infty$$

The zero position, 0, represents nothing relative to all the other numbers, which represent something. It also represents the position of the one using the numbers, the mathematician, the person, the absolute of numbers. The number line symbolizes the infinite continuum of positive and negative quality numbers from one to infinity. The numbers exist relative to their absolute source-cause, a thinking, choosing, using *personality*.

You have probably heard it asked: Which came first, the chicken or the egg? The answer is: neither. What comes first in infinity is an infinite, eternal, and universal **absolute**, an antecedent Source-Cause; in actuality, the one and only Uncaused Cause in infinity. The will of **this Person** is the infinite, absolute, and eternal singularity, which is ancestral to every absolute and every relativity in infinity. It is only natural to qualify this absolute singularity as the will of God, the first person of infinity. $1 = \infty$ is the symbolic representation of *GOD*, the most common name given to this unnamed entity and source-cause of infinity, a Person.

23

A *Person* is the Source of every thing, meaning, value, and personality in infinity? Right! If you are a person and I am a person, how could the Source of Persons be anything *less* than a person or anyone other than the First Person and Source of Everything and every other person? This first person comes before names or numbers, and I now relate to this Person as my personal spiritual Father, **God**, the Person who endowed me with free will, self-consciousness, mind, and spirit.

As an atheist, I had finally come to the conclusion that, in reality, there *is* a God, albeit a God far transcending the traditional concepts of Christianity derived largely from the Bible and the institutional religions of fear. **$1 = \infty$**! Was this the unified field equation that Dr. Einstein had long sought and died trying to find? How could it be anything else? It was true, there *is* a God of science who I could know and love for having made me and everything and everyone else possible.

This was a mind-blowing time of my life, February of 1969, in Penngrove, California! The last thing or person I expected to discover as a scientist was God. I was a hard-core atheist, but I was also an eclectic, one who loved truth. I was happy to take it from any source that revealed it. The jackpot of my life had paid off in spite of my having been set-up, falsely accused, arrested, framed, and fired as a teacher over felony charges for marijuana possession. There **was** a God, and I was so happy to have found him I could hardly stand it!!

24

I tried to put myself in Einstein's shoes. What would he have done if he had concluded the unified field theory and derived the unified field equation before he died? I concluded that he would have written a paper on the subject, but first, because of the potentials of the political application inherent in the equation and the fact that the Vietnam War was raging, I decided I should inform the President as a matter of national security. After all, $E = mc^2$ had brought us the bomb, and I knew that the political application of the unified field equation, $\mathbf{1} = \infty$, could bring an end to the war in southeast Asia and peace to our world for the benefit of every man, woman, and child on earth.

Richard Milhaus Nixon was President of the United States at the time, and in March of 1969, I called the White House and attempted to make an appointment with the President to inform him that the Unified Field Equation long sought by Dr. Einstein had been completed. The political application of this reality to the Vietnam War could have brought an end to hostilities in such a way as to avoid any *loss of face* to either or any side. Science had discovered the fact that there *is* a God of love and law and order! And because each of us on earth exists in relation to this same *Infinite Person* and are all related to this Primal Person equally and in the same way, we are all related to each other. Two or more persons related to another person are all related to each other.

Every man, woman, and child on earth is a unique personal version of exactly the same thing: a son or daughter of God! The family of God includes every man, woman, and child on earth. The spiritual brotherhood of all humankind is based on the recognition of the Fatherhood of God. The Fatherhood of God is the foundation of the brotherhood of all humankind.

The brotherhood of man is predicated on the recognition of the fatherhood of God. Mutual understanding and fraternal love are transcendent civilizers and mighty factors in the worldwide realization of the brotherhood of man. And the quickest way to realize the brotherhood of man on earth today is to effect the spiritual transformation of present-day humanity.

Shortly after I began writing a paper on the unified field equation, a visiting friend asked me to listen to something he had found in a new book he had just discovered, *The Urantia Book*. And he read something to me from a paper titled: ENERGY—MIND AND MATTER. Whatever it was blew my mind! It was too good to be true! The information was too new and too advanced to be in print! I had just made the second greatest discovery of my life, *The Urantia Book*. I soon realized I was reading the greatest cosmology every written on earth. It unified science, philosophy, and religion. It filled in all the missing links in my chain of knowledge and understanding of how things had come to be the way they are in the universe and on earth.

I soon concluded that it would be ridiculous for me to write something on the cosmology of the unified field equation when ***it was all there in The Urantia Book***! I could never explain it as well as it is written throughout the book, especially in Paper 105—*DEITY AND REALITY*. And ever since that day, I have sought to introduce people to God and *The Urantia Book*. Without the gift of *The Urantia Book*, I don't think we would survive as a global group of human beings.

Then along comes George W. Bush, and he becomes President of the United States under some shady and assertive circumstances. He then inaugurates a new national and foreign policy of preemptive attacks on presumed enemies with a war in Iraq, and everything changed radically for the worse. The people of Iraq now have in common with the people of Japan, Diego Garcia, Afghanistan, Korea, and Hawai'i the fact that their nation is occupied by the same military force of the same government that has overthrown and occupied many countries during the course of its political evolution.

America has become a very dangerous, rogue government in a very dangerous position. This nation has more weapons of mass destruction, more atomic, biological, and chemical weapons, and more weapons delivery systems than any nation on earth. Not only does the President take the people into a so-called war on terrorism where the punishment exceeds the crime and the action is against the will of God, The

Law of Nations, and the U. S. Constitution, he does so unlawfully and without just cause, adding to his list of mass murders while claiming victory for his gross misdeeds.

And according to the pollsters, over 70% of the American people clapped their hands and cheered him on, loving him for what he has done in spite of all of the laws of man and God that have been broken in the process of his destructive attack against the Rule of Law, Love, and Truth. President Bush has grossly violated the Golden Rule of Living, doing to other people and their nation what he would never want done to himself or his nation. So with a President in rebellion and with control over the most destructive arsenal and delivery systems ever created on earth, we have a situation far worse than what we contemplated would happen if Hitler got the bomb first!

The people of America and the world are face to face with the problem of having a criminally insane President supported by criminally insane advisers who appear hell-bent on creating a religious war between Christians and Moslems in the process of creating their new Empire of Oil and Gas Producing Nations under the clouds of fear produced by the anti-terrorists and their friends. And this is where the long train of abuses and usurpations has brought us, perpetrated by a continuum of leaders of the U. S. government, pursuing invariably the same object, evincing a design to reduce us under absolute Despotism.

III. THE WAY OUT

For well over one hundred years, the U. S. government has pursued policies that violate The Law of Nations and made choices that violate the U. S. Constitution and abrogate Article Six, Sections 2 and 3 of the Supremacy Clause. So many presidents, senators, representatives, governors, judges, and other officials in the executive, legislative, and judicial branches of the U. S. and state governments have made so many choices that are inconsistent with the Preamble and Article Six, Sections 2 and 3 of the U. S. Constitution, violations of The Law of Nations, the Golden Rule, and the will of God without getting caught or having to answer for it, as to render the Constitution of the United States null and void. It has become something that is only *pretended* to be followed and true by all those who made choices that betrayed their trust and abrogated Article Six of the U. S. Constitution.

Americans claim to be God-knowing, God-fearing people. They have all been taught that they should be perfect, even as God is perfect, that they should love one another, and that they should not kill one another. They believe they can do no wrong because they believe the philosophy that might makes right, and they are the favored nation. It's o.k. for them to kill the bad guys since they are the good guys! What a joke!

30

They don't know they suffer from *KDS*, knowledge deficiency syndrome. They would never make it to world peace without a road map.

World peace includes personal peace, moral peace, social peace, economic peace, and political peace. World peace means no more deaths by starvation, and no one goes to bed hungry anymore. The secret of a better civilization is bound up in the education and enlightenment of the individual. World peace means an end to all forms of war and slavery. World peace means a paradigm shift from the dangers of militant nationalism to the green pastures of globalism concomitant with a new form of world government of all mankind, by all mankind, and for all mankind and all nations. A new form of democratic, representative world government of the people, by the people, and for the people and the nations of the world implies the eventual selection of an ideal location, somewhere on earth, to serve as the capitol and administrative center of the government of the people and the nations of the world.

World peace is an attainable global reality, just as attainable and deliverable as the atomic bomb or world wars. A knowledge and understanding of the unified field equation, $1 = \infty$ and a copy of *The Urantia Book*, is all that is necessary for the acquirement of personal peace in today's world. What the people of the world need most to know in common is the fact that God is their Father, and the truth is that they are the sons and daughters of God. By faith, they can actually realize and daily experience this ennobling truth. We are all here on the same planet, warmed by the same sun, shined on by the same moon, living in the same solar system in the same galaxy in the same infinite universe, and we are all loved and endowed by the same Infinite Person, our Father, **GOD**. And forget not: establishing world peace is far cheaper than waging world wars.

See if the following information on *Sovereignty, Divine, and Human* rings your truth bell. You have to become truth-coordinated to make it from here to world peace, so follow the Spirit of Truth to the on-ramp of the pathway of infinite perfection and read the following essential information. On page 1486 of *The Urantia Book*, it is revealed that "The brotherhood of man is founded on the Fatherhood of God. The family of God is derived from the love of God—God is love. God the Father divinely loves his children, all of them."

"The kingdom of heaven, the divine government, is founded on the fact of divine sovereignty — God is spirit. Since God is spirit, this kingdom is spiritual. The kingdom of heaven is neither material nor merely intellectual; it is a spiritual relationship between God and man."

"If different religions recognize the spirit sovereignty of God the Father, then will all such religions remain at peace.

Only when one religion assumes that it is in some way superior to all others and that it possesses exclusive authority over other religions, will such a religion presume to be intolerant of other religions or dare to persecute other religious believers."

"Religious peace — brotherhood — can never exist unless all religions are willing to completely divest themselves of all ecclesiastical authority and fully surrender all concept of spiritual sovereignty. God alone is spirit sovereign."

"You cannot have equality among religions (religious liberty) without having religious wars unless all religions consent to the transfer of all religious sovereignty to some superhuman level, to God Himself."

"The kingdom of heaven in the hearts of men will create religious unity (not necessarily uniformity) because any and all religious groups composed of such religious believers will be free from all notion of ecclesiastical authority — religious sovereignty."

"God is spirit, and God gives a fragment of his spirit self to dwell in the heart of man. Spiritually, all men are equal. The kingdom of heaven is free from castes, classes, social levels, and economic groups. You are all brethren."

"But the moment you lose sight of the spirit sovereignty of God the Father, someone religion will begin to assert its superiority over other religions; and then, instead of peace on earth and good will among men, there will start dissensions, recriminations, even religious wars, at least wars among religionists."

"Freewill beings who regard themselves as equals, unless they mutually acknowledge themselves as subject to some super-sovereignty, some authority over and above themselves, sooner or later are tempted to try out their ability to gain power and authority over other persons and groups. The concept of equality never brings peace except in the mutual recognition of some over-controlling influence of super-sovereignty."

"There can be no lasting religious peace on earth until all religious groups freely surrender all their notions of divine favor, chosen people, and religious sovereignty. ...Only when God the Father becomes supreme will men become religious brothers and live together in religious peace on earth."

We are at a peculiarly critical stage of the evolution of political sovereignty in this twentieth century after Christ. The following section of the road map to world peace is essential to an objective understanding of political sovereignty.

"War will never end on (earth) so long as nations cling to the illusive notions of unlimited national sovereignty. There are only two levels of relative sovereignty on an inhabited world: the spiritual free will of the individual mortal and the collective sovereignty of mankind as a whole. Between the level of the individual human being and the level of the total of mankind, all groupings and associations are relative, transitory, and of value only in so far as they enhance the welfare, well-being, and progress of the individual and the planetary grand total — man and mankind."

"Religious teachers must always remember that the spiritual sovereignty of God overrides all intervening and intermediate spiritual loyalties. Someday civil rulers will learn that the Most Highs rule in the kingdoms of men."

"This rule of the Most Highs in the kingdoms of men is not for the especial benefit of any especially favored group of mortals. There is no such thing as a "chosen people." The rule of the Most Highs, the over-controllers of political evolution, is a rule designed to foster the greatest good to the greatest number of all men and for the greatest length of time."

"Sovereignty is power and it grows by organization. This growth of the organization of political power is good and proper, for it tends to encompass ever-widening segments of the total of mankind. But this same growth of political organizations creates a problem at every intervening stage between the initial and natural organization of political power — the family — and the final consummation of political growth — the government of all mankind, by all mankind, and for all mankind."

"Starting out with parental power in the family group, political sovereignty evolves by organization as families overlap into consanguineous clans which become united, for various reasons, into tribal units — superconsanguineous political groupings. And then, by trade, commerce, and conquest, tribes become unified as a nation, while nations themselves sometimes become unified by empire."

"As sovereignty passes from smaller groups to larger groups, wars are lessened. That is, minor wars between smaller nations are lessened, but the potential for greater wars is increased as the nations wielding sovereignty become larger and larger. When all the world has been explored and occupied, when nations are few, strong, and powerful, when these great and supposedly sovereign nations come to touch borders, when only oceans separate them, then will the stage be set for major wars, world-wide conflicts. So-called sovereign nations cannot rub elbows without generating conflicts and eventuating wars."

"The difficulty in the evolution of political sovereignty from the family to all mankind, lies in the inertia-resistance exhibited on all intervening levels. Families have, on occasion, defied their clan, while clans and tribes have often been subversive of the sovereignty of the territorial state. Each new and forward evolution of political sovereignty is (and has always been) embarrassed and hampered by the "scaffolding stages" of the previous developments in political organization. And this is true because human loyalties, once mobilized, are hard to change. The same loyalty which makes possible the evolution of the tribe, makes difficult the evolution of the supertribe — the territorial state. And the same loyalty (patriotism) which makes possible the evolution of the territorial state, vastly complicates the evolutionary development of the government of all mankind."

"Political sovereignty is created out of the surrender of self-determinism, first by the individual within the family and then by the families and clans in relation to the tribe and larger groupings. This progressive transfer of self-determination from the smaller to ever larger political organizations has generally proceeded unabated in the East since the establishment of the Ming and the Mogul dynasties. In the West it obtained for more than a thousand years right on down to the end of (World War I), when an unfortunate retrograde movement temporarily reversed this normal trend by reestablishing the submerged political sovereignty of numerous small groups in Europe."

"(Our world) will not enjoy lasting peace until the so-called sovereign nations intelligently and fully surrender their sovereign powers into the hands of the brotherhood of men — mankind government. Internationalism — Leagues of Nations — can never bring permanent peace to mankind. World-wide confederations of nations will effectively prevent minor wars and acceptably control the smaller nations, but they will not prevent world wars nor control the three, four, or five most powerful governments. In the face of real conflicts, one of these world powers will withdraw from the League and declare war. You cannot prevent nations going to war as long as they remain infected with the delusional virus of national sovereignty. Internationalism is a step in the right direction. An international police force will prevent many minor wars, but it will not be effective in preventing major wars, conflicts between the great military governments of earth."

"As the number of truly sovereign nations (great powers) decreases, so do both opportunity and need for mankind government increase. When there are only a few really sovereign (great) powers, either they must embark on the life and death struggle for national (imperial) supremacy, or else, by voluntary surrender of certain prerogatives of sovereignty, they must create the essential nucleus of supernational power which will serve as the beginning of the real sovereignty of all mankind."

"Peace will not come to (our planet) until every so-called sovereign nation surrenders its power to make war into the hands of a representative government of all mankind. Political sovereignty is innate with the peoples of the world. When all the peoples of the planet create a world government, they have the right and the power to make such a government SOVEREIGN; and when such a representative or democratic world power controls the world's land, air, and naval forces, peace on earth and good will among men can prevail — but not until then."

"To use an important nineteenth- and twentieth-century illustration: The (various) states of the American Federal Union have long enjoyed peace. They have no more wars among themselves. They have surrendered their sovereignty to the federal government, and through the arbitrament of war, they have abandoned all claims to the delusions of self-determination. While each state regulates its internal affairs, it is not concerned with foreign relations, tariffs, immigration, military affairs, or interstate commerce. Neither do the individual states concern themselves with matters of citizenship. The various states suffer the ravages of war only when the federal government's sovereignty is in some way jeopardized."

"These (fifty) states, having abandoned the twin sophistries of sovereignty and self-determination, enjoy interstate peace and tranquility. So will the nations of the world begin to enjoy peace when they freely surrender their respective sovereignties into the hands of a global government — the sovereignty of the brotherhood of men. In this world state (an environment of political equality will be attained), the small nations will be as powerful as the great, even as the small state of Rhode Island has its two senators in the American Congress just the same as the populous state of New York or the large state of Texas."

"The limited (state) sovereignty of these various states was created by men and for men. The superstate (national) sovereignty of the American Federal Union was created by the original thirteen of these states for their own benefit and for the benefit of men. Sometime the supernational sovereignty of the planetary government of mankind will be similarly created by nations for their own benefit and for the benefit of all men."

"Citizens are not born for the benefit of governments; governments are organizations created and devised for the benefit of men. There can be no end to the evolution of political sovereignty short of the appearance of the government of the sovereignty of all men. All other sovereignties are relative in value, intermediate in meaning, and subordinate in status."

"With scientific progress, wars are going to become more and more devastating until they become almost racially suicidal. How many world wars must be fought and how many leagues of nations must fail before men will be willing to establish the government of mankind and begin to enjoy the blessings of permanent peace and thrive on the tranquility of good will — world-wide good will — among men?"

We can't afford to wait any longer to effect the consummation of political evolution through the creation of a new form of representative world government of the people, by the people, and for the people and nations of the world. The following section on law, liberty, and sovereignty explains just what we need to know to achieve our goal of world peace.

"If one man craves freedom — liberty — he must remember that all other men long for the same freedom. Groups of such liberty-loving mortals cannot live together in peace without becoming subservient to such laws, rules, and regulations as will grant each person the same degree of freedom while at the same time safeguarding an equal degree of freedom for all of his fellow mortals. If one man is to be absolutely free, then another must become an absolute slave. And the relative nature of freedom is true socially, economically, and politically. Freedom is the gift of civilization made possible by the enforcement of LAW."

"Religion makes it spiritually possible to realize the brotherhood of men, but it will require mankind government to regulate the social, economic, and political problems associated with such a goal of human happiness and efficiency."

"There shall be wars and rumors of wars — nation will rise against nation — just as long as the world's political sovereignty is divided up and unjustly held by a group of nation-states. England, Scotland, and Wales were always fighting each other until they gave up their respective sovereignties, reposing them in the United Kingdom."

(World War II taught us to form the United Nations Organization, thus creating the machinery for preventing small wars, wars between the lesser nations. But the United Nations Organization simply isn't good enough.) "Global wars will go on until the government of mankind is created. Global sovereignty will prevent global wars — nothing else can." (The diverse American free states live together in peace.) "There are among the citizens of all these states, all of the various nationalities and races that live in the ever-warring nations of Europe. These Americans represent almost all the religions and religious sects and cults of the whole wide world, and yet here in North America they live together in peace. And all this is made possible because all of these states have surrendered their sovereignty and have abandoned all notions of the supposed rights of self-determination."

"It is not a question of armaments or disarmament. Neither does the question of conscription or voluntary military service enter into these problems of maintaining world-wide peace. If you take every form of modern mechanical armaments and all types of explosives away from strong nations, they will fight with fists, stones, and clubs as long as they cling to their delusions of the divine right of national sovereignty. War is not man's great and terrible disease; war is a symptom, a result. The real disease is the virus of national sovereignty."

"The nations of our planet have not possessed real sovereignty; they never have had a sovereignty which could protect them from the ravages and devastations of world wars. In the creation of the global government of mankind the nations are not giving up sovereignty so much as they are actually creating a real, bona fide, and lasting world sovereignty which will henceforth be fully able to protect them from all war. Local affairs will be handled by local governments; national affairs, by national governments; international affairs will be administered by global government.

"World peace cannot be maintained by treaties, diplomacy, foreign policies, alliances, balances power, or any other type of makeshift juggling with the sovereignties of nationalism. World law must come into being and must be enforced by world government — the sovereignty of all mankind."

"The individual will enjoy far more liberty under world government. Today, the citizens of the great powers are taxed, regulated, and controlled almost oppressively, and much of this present interference with individual liberties will vanish when the national governments are willing to trustee their sovereignty as regards international affairs into the hands of global government."

"Under global government the national groups will be afforded a real opportunity to realize and enjoy the personal liberties of genuine democracy. The fallacy of self-determination will be ended. With global regulation of money and trade will come the new era of world-wide peace. Soon may a global language evolve, and there will be at least some hope of sometime having a global religion — or religions with a global viewpoint."

"Collective security will never afford peace until the collectivity includes all mankind."

"The political sovereignty of representative mankind government will bring lasting peace on earth, and the spiritual brotherhood of man will forever insure good will among all men. And there is no other way whereby peace on earth and good will among men can be realized."

To further participate in the Divine Conspiracy to save us from ourselves and the potentials of group destruction, I believe that a Global Constitutional Convention is essential to the creation of a Master Charter of Liberty, a Constitution of World Law for the government of the people and the nations of the world.

The Road Map to World Peace shows a route that begins and ends in Hawai'i. What do the people of Japan, Korea, Diego Garcia, Afghanistan, Iraq, and Hawai'i all have in common besides spiritual brotherhood? Their nation is **Occupied** by the military forces of **the same de facto government** of the United States! Their governments were all overthrown by machinations of the government of the United States of America; Hawai'i has been illegally occupied since January 17th, 1893, following an illegal act of war in violation of The Law of Nations and the United States Constitution.

Since Operation Crossroads in 1946, the United States Government has been taking the people of the world past the crossroads that lead to **World Peace and the Pits of Global Destruction**. Since the preemptive war with Iraq and the invasion and occupation of Iraq by a coalition willing to follow the United States and Great Britain away from the rule of law, into rebellion against the will of God and the law of the universe, the consequences of this great mistake are now beginning to show the real intents and purposes of the <u>oil, gas and water pirates</u> who all conspired together to pull-off another theft of natural resources and political sovereignty in the history of a long career of a continuing, on-going criminal enterprise made up of a long train of abuses of power and usurpations of rights that abrogate Article VI, Sections 2 and 3 of the U. S. Constitution.

The U. S. Road Map for Peace in the Middle East will only lead to more war because it simply isn't good enough. It ignores too many facts and truths about the Jewish people and the Middle East and is too self-serving of American—British interests. **Israel should not be recognized** as a reinstated nation under the Rule of <u>Postliminium</u> because the government of the Israelis was completely overthrown and destroyed by the Roman armies in A.D. 70. The reason for the overthrow of the Jews and their nation was the rejection and murder of Jesus, the incarnate Creator of the Universe of our residence, which abrogated the Divine Covenant between God and man established with Abraham by Machiventa Melchizedek nearly two-thousand years before the seventh and final bestowal and material incarnation of Jesus of Nazareth.

The cause behind all this has to do with the fact that the Sovereign of the System of spheres to which our world belongs and the Planetary Prince of our planet initiated a rebellion against the government of the Universe and the will of God. The **Lucifer Rebellion** was launched with a so-called declaration of liberty about two hundred thousand years ago, and Satan, the top lieutenant of Lucifer, advocated the cause of the rebellion on earth. The rebel Planetary Prince of our planet, Caligastia, is the so-called "Devil" who bought into Lucifer's assumptions of self-assertion, and our world has been isolated by rebellion and quarantined in communicado ever since.

The Creator-Father of our universe chose to incarnate on our world as a means of reinstating the Law and Order of Universe Government for our world of confusion, chaos, and rebellion. The problems associated with our existence on earth are impossible of understanding without a knowledge of certain great epochs of the past, especially the occurrence and consequences of the planetary rebellion (see pp 754-762, *The Urantia Book*). This rebellion did not seriously interfere with the progress of organic evolution, but it did radically interfere with the course of social evolution and spiritual development, profoundly influencing the superphysical history of our world.

When I was an atheist, I used to think that there could be no God because I thought he wouldn't have allowed man to be exposed to so much negative quality reality over the years. But that was when I was unconscious of the fact that I had been given the power and responsibility of freewill choice. I didn't know that every issue of personal conduct is a matter of freewill choice. I had yet to acquire any cosmic identity or wisdom. How could I possibly have understood the cosmic situation we are all in on this world?

(We have found it difficult fully) "to comprehend the significance and grasp the meanings of evil, error, sin, and iniquity. (We have) been slow to perceive that contrastive perfection and imperfection produce potential evil; that conflicting truth and falsehood create confusing error; that the divine endowment of freewill choice eventuates in the divergent realms of sin and righteousness. We have failed to realize that the persistent pursuit of divinity leads to the kingdom of God, in contrast with its on-going rejection, which leads to the domains of iniquity."

"Evil is not created by God nor does God permit sin and rebellion. Potential evil is time-existent in a universe which embraces differential levels of perfection meanings and values. Sin is potential where and when imperfect persons are endowed with the ability to choose between good and evil. The potentiality of error is bound up in the conflicting presence of truth and untruth, fact and falsehood. The deliberate choice of evil constitutes sin, while the willful rejection of truth is error, and the persistent pursuit of sin and error is iniquity." (p 613, *The Urantia Book*)

"There are many ways of looking at sin, but from the universe philosophic viewpoint sin is the attitude of a personality who is knowingly resisting cosmic reality."

"Sin must be redefined as deliberate disloyalty to Deity. There are degrees of disloyalty: the partial loyalty of indecision; the divided loyalty of confliction; the dying loyalty of indifference; and the death of loyalty exhibited in devotion to godless ideals."

"The sense or feeling of guilt is the consciousness of the violation of the mores; it is not necessarily sin. There is no real sin in the absence of conscious disloyalty to Deity." (see p 984, *The Urantia Book*)

One evening, in response to questions from his apostles who wanted to know: "Master, what is evil?" Jesus said:

"Make clear in your mind these different attitudes toward the Father and His universe. Never forget these laws of relation to the Father's will:"

"Evil is the unconscious or unintended transgression of the divine law, the Father's will. Evil is likewise the measure of the imperfectness of obedience to the Father's will."

"Sin is the conscious, knowing, and deliberate transgression of the divine law, the Father's will. Sin is the measure of unwillingness to be divinely led and spiritually directed."

"Iniquity is the willful, determined, and persistent transgression of the divine law, the Father's will. Iniquity is the measure of the continued rejection of the Father's loving plan of personality survival and the Sons' merciful ministry of salvation."

"By nature, before the rebirth of the spirit, mortal man is subject to inherent evil tendencies, but such natural imperfections of behavior are neither sin nor iniquity. Mortal man is just beginning his long ascent to the perfection of the Father in Paradise. To be imperfect or partial in natural endowment is not sinful. Man is indeed subject to evil, but he is in no sense the child of the evil one unless he has knowingly and deliberately chosen the paths of sin and the life of iniquity. Evil is inherent in the natural order of this world, but sin is an attitude of conscious rebellion which was brought to this world by those who fell from spiritual light into gross darkness."

Perhaps now you are beginning to see how important it is to know that you have been endowed by God with the power of freewill choice, that you have the power to choose between the attitudes of good and evil, that every issue of personal or group conduct is a matter of freewill choice, and every choice is made in relation to the will of God, which *is* the law of the universe. If you want to begin making things more the way they ought to be on this planet, then you must begin to make choices that are conscious and consistent, rather than inconsistent, with the will of God. The will of God is living love and truth. The quality of your thinking, talking, acting, reacting, and analysis of the consequences of your choosing is faithfully reflected in the fruits of the spirit which are yielded in the lives of spirit-born, God-knowing human beings, including: *loving service, unselfish devotion, courageous loyalty, sincere fairness, enlightened honesty, undying hope, confiding trust, merciful ministry, unfailing goodness, forgiving tolerance, and enduring peace.*

It may help to know something about the age we are in now, the epoch known as the Post-Bestowal Son Man Age. On page 589 of *The Urantia Book*, seven planetary mortal epochs are revealed, and our current age is described on pp 597-598 under *Urantia's Postbestowal Age*, which I here include in its entirety:

"The bestowal Son is the Prince of Peace (for our world, it was Jesus). He arrives with the message, 'Peace on earth and good will among men.' On normal worlds this is a dispensation of world-wide peace; the nations no more learn war. But such salutary influences did not attend the coming of your bestowal Son, Christ Michael. Urantia is not proceeding in the normal order. Your world is out of step in the planetary procession. Your Master, when on earth, warned his disciples that his advent would not bring the usual reign of peace on Urantia. He distinctly told them that there would be 'wars and rumors of wars,' and that nation would rise against nation. At another time he said, 'Think not that I have come to bring peace upon earth.'"

"Even on normal evolutionary worlds the realization of the world-wide brotherhood of man is not an easy accomplishment. On a confused and disordered planet like Urantia such an achievement requires a much longer time and necessitates far greater effort. Unaided social evolution can hardly achieve such happy results on a spiritually isolated sphere. Religious revelation is essential to the realization of brotherhood on Urantia. While Jesus has shown the way to the immediate attainment of spiritual brotherhood, the realization of social brotherhood on your world depends much on the achievement of the following personal transformations and planetary adjustments:"

"1. Social fraternity. Multiplication of international and interracial social contacts and fraternal associations through travel, commerce, and competitive play. Development of a common language and the multiplication of multilinguists. The racial and national interchange of students, teachers, industrialists, and religious philosophers."

"2. Intellectual cross-fertilization. Brotherhood is impossible on a world whose inhabitants are so primitive that they fail to recognize the folly of unmitigated selfishness. There must occur an exchange of national and racial literature. Each race must become familiar with the thought of all races; each nation must know the feelings of all nations. Ignorance breeds suspicion, and suspicion is incompatible with the essential attitude of sympathy and love."

"3. Ethical awakening. Only ethical consciousness can unmask the immorality of human intolerance and the sinfulness of fratricidal strife. Only a moral conscience can condemn the evils of national envy and racial jealousy. Only moral beings will ever seek for that spiritual insight which is essential to living the golden rule."

"4. Political wisdom. Emotional maturity is essential to self-control. Only emotional maturity will insure the substitution of international techniques of civilized adjudication for the barbarous arbitrament of war. Wise statesmen will sometime work for the welfare of humanity even while they strive to promote the interest of their national or racial groups. Selfish political sagacity is ultimately suicidal — destructive of all those enduring qualities which insure planetary group survival."

"5. Spiritual insight. The brotherhood of man is, after all, predicated on the recognition of the fatherhood of God. The quickest way to realize the brotherhood of man on Urantia is to effect the spiritual transformation of present-day humanity. The only technique for accelerating the natural trend of social evolution is that of applying spiritual pressure from above, thus augmenting moral insight while enhancing the soul capacity of every mortal to understand and love every other mortal. Mutual understanding and fraternal love are transcendent civilizers and mighty factors in the world-wide realization of the brotherhood of man."

"If you could be transplanted from your backward and confused world to some normal planet now in the *postbestowal* Son age, you would think you had been translated to the heaven of your traditions. You would hardly believe that you were observing the normal evolutionary workings of a mortal sphere of human habitation. These worlds are in the spiritual circuits of their realm, and they enjoy all the advantages of the universe broadcasts and the reflectivity services of the superuniverse."

You are personally *equipped* to recognize the fact, the law, and the love of God, and it is important that you become increasingly truth-coordinated if you want to enjoy personal peace and increasing happiness as a component of social, moral, economic, and political peace. As a son or daughter of God on this planet, you have been endowed with the living spirit of the Prince of Peace, the Spirit of Truth, which **enshrouds** the soul within one's mind. This is sort of like your *Jesus Gene*. The *God Gene,* the endowment of the perfect spirit of the Universal Father, is one quantum unit of the will of God **within** the soul of man. And if you follow the leading of these spirit endowments, you will become increasingly perfect, *increasingly God-like*, and increasingly happy.

Your relationship with these indwelling spirit entities *is* the kingdom of heaven. Heaven is everywhere God is, and since the spirit of God is within your mind and soul, the kingdom of heaven is within you. You may enjoy an instant and on-going access to the Creator of the Universe of our residence and the Universal Father of Paradise. If you dare to simply believe that God loves you with an infinite love, you will find yourself in the kingdom of God. The kingdom of God is the will of God, dominant and transcendent in the heart of the believer in *sonship* with God and brotherhood with all humankind.

Thus the Road Map for World Peace reveals the truth of a spiritual approach to the resolution of our personal, social, moral, economic, and political problems on earth. The worldwide realization of the Fatherhood of God and personal recognition of the spiritual brotherhood of all human beings is basic to the attainment of personal, social, moral, economic, and political peace on earth. The attainment of world peace requires the creation of a new form of world government of all humankind, by all humankind, and for all humankind and all nations. And to get there from here in today's world requires nothing less than a Global Constitutional Convention to create a Master Charter of Liberty, a Constitution of World Law for the People and the Government of all Humankind.

This is NOT the so-called New World Order talked about by President George W. Bush and all of his rich and powerful friends who *own* the U. S. government *and* the Central Bank of America, the Federal Reserve System. I am not talking about a world government of the few, by the few, and for the few who would gladly assert their will over you, me, *or* God. And I am not talking about the United Nations Organization, a **Soviet** political instrumentality, a negative quality form of world government, which *is* the New World Order of the moment.

In his book "Masters of Deceit," J. Edgar Hoover reveals that the word *soviet* means a council or commission made up of people who have been appointed, not elected to office. The United Nations Organization is made up of nothing but councils and commissions, including the general assembly, and none of them are made up of people who have been elected to office by the general electorate. It is a negative quality Soviet political instrumentality that the New World Order Gang have been using to pass resolutions as part of the process of establishing the authority of a New World **Empire** of Gas and Oil Producing Nations contrary to the Golden Rule of Living, the Law of the Universe, and the will of God.

Presidents Bush and their friends, who constitute a vicious minority of people entrenched behind political, financial, and ecclesiastical power, should not be permitted to further organize themselves for the exploitation and oppression of those who, because of their idealism, are not disposed to resort to force for self-protection or for the furtherance of their laudable life projects. The Creator of our universe detests commercializing the practices of religion as well as all forms of unfairness and profiteering at the expense of the poor and the unlearned. Jesus does not look with approval upon the refusal to employ force to protect the majority of any given human group against the unfair and enslaving practices of unjust minorities such as the big five nations who have reduced the rest of the people and nations of the world to political inequality, global political slavery.

Representatives of the people and the nations of the world must unite in a Global Constitutional Convention to create a Master Charter of Liberty if they want to liberate themselves from the fetters of political and spiritual incompleteness on the frontiers of international and global reality. The creation of this document and its ratification by the people and nations of the world is fundamental to the future of freedom and the establishment of peace on earth and good will among all men.

The delegates to this Convention could, for example, choose to make war and all weapons of mass destruction illegal. And since we are all God's children and the natural resources of this world are actually gifts from God for the equal benefit of the entire human family, the delegates could decide to "globalize" the natural resources of the world so each member of the brotherhood of all humankind could get their fair share of the family's natural wealth. For example, if oil and natural gas were "globalized" rather than nationalized or owned by a few individuals, every man, woman, and child on earth could get their fair share of any income derived from the sale or use of the oil and gas of the world. No one would be broke anymore, and no one would have to go to bed hungry for lack of food for lack of money.

A Global Constitutional Convention could also decide to create a Global Bank for the government of the people and the nations of the world. The economic unification of the central banks of the world by the Treasury of the Government of all Humankind would be fundamental to global economic reorganization, economic peace, and global economic freedom.

Under a global government good enough for everyone and every nation, the people and nations of the world could have equal access to judicial authority and peaceful adjudicative resolution. International disputes and complaints could be adjudicated by civilized and peaceful means. Temporary restraining orders could keep one nation from occupying another nation or nations if world government and world law enforced them.

Political freedom based on political equality and spiritual freedom based on spiritual equality would raise every person and every nation to heretofore-unattained levels of spiritual and political equalityand freedom. With the spiritual unification of the human race, the political reorganization of the people of the world under the sovereignty of a New Form of World Government of all mankind, by all mankind, and for all mankind and all nations becomes a real possibility and global disarmament of all weapons of mass destruction can be righteously attained.

The group of all humankind must experience the worldwide realization of the spiritual brotherhood as soon as it can be effected because it opens the door to personal, social, moral, economic, and political peace on earth while burying all the fears of nationalism, hate, and war. War is the heritage of early evolutionary man who has yet to realize the truth of sonship with God and brotherhood with all men. Physical combat as a technique of adjusting racial misunderstandings must become a thing of the past.

In a masterful discussion of True and False Liberty on page 613 of *The Urantia Book*, it is revealed that "true liberty is the associate of genuine self-respect; false liberty the consort of self-admiration. True liberty is the fruit of self-control; false liberty, the assumption of self-assertion. Self-control leads to altruistic service; self-admiration tends towards the exploitation of others for the selfish aggrandizement of such a mistaken individual as is willing to sacrifice righteous attainment for the sake of possessing unjust power over his fellow beings."

"Even wisdom is divine and safe only when it is cosmic in scope and spiritual in motivation."

"There is no error greater than that species of self-deception which leads intelligent beings to crave the exercise of power over other beings for the purpose of depriving these persons of their natural liberties. The golden rule of human fairness cries out against all such fraud, unfairness, selfishness, and unrighteousness. Only true and genuine liberty is compatible with the reign of love and the ministry of mercy."

"How dare the self-willed creature encroach upon the rights of his fellows in the name of personal liberty when the Supreme Rulers of the universe stand back in merciful respect for these prerogatives of will and potentials of personality! No being, in the exercise of his supposed personal liberty, has a right to deprive any other being of those privileges of existence conferred by the Creators and duly respected by all their loyal associates, subordinates, and subjects..."

"No being in all the universe has the rightful liberty to deprive any other being of true liberty, the right to love and be loved, the privilege of worshiping God and of serving his fellows."

Brothers and sisters of the world: the Kingdom of God is at hand! And I say this in Hawai'i where the Kingdom of Hawai'i has been reinstated as the lawful, de jure government of Hawai'i in the midst of the de facto State of Hawai'i and the de facto U. S. government. At this moment of time and in this space, it is literally true: *the Kingdom of God and the Kingdom of Hawai'i are both at hand!*

For those of you who are not aware of the history of Hawai'i, it is important for you to know that Hawai'i was an independent, internationally recognized nation when it was overthrown by an illegal act of war on January 17, 1893, by the same government that now occupies Japan, Korea, Diego Garcia, Afghanistan, and Iraq in addition to Hawai'i. At that time, the United States Government wanted Pearl Harbor as a base of operations for their sovereignty-wielding escapades in the Pacific Region.

The Kingdom of Hawai'i had treaties with the United States and more than thirty other independent nations. All these were broken when U. S. government officials betrayed the trust of their oath sworn under Article Six, Section 3 of the U. S. Constitution and abrogated Article Six, Section 2 of the same Constitution. The consequences of this gross misuse and abuse of power were the usurpation of the rights of the American officials and the usurpation of the rights of the people and government of the Kingdom of Hawai'i.

The Kingdom of Hawai'i was forced into exile by an illegal provisional government. The U. S. government unlawfully received all the natural resources and lands belonging to the people and Government of Hawai'i when the provisional government illegally ceded them to the U. S. government. It is unlawful to steal, and it is unlawful to sell stolen properties.

After 100 years of exile in America, President William J. Clinton and the U. S. Congress signed off on Public Law 103-150, the so-called Apology Bill. The natural consequences of this action revealed the potential of Hawaiian independence and the reinstatement of the lawful Government of Hawai'i under national and international law. This public law is here included because of its importance to the adjudication of the Case of Liliuokalani vs. the U. S. government and the reinstatement of her government under the international Rule of Postliminium in The Law of Nations (p 313):

UNITED STATES PUBLIC LAW 103-150
103d Congress Joint Resolution 19

Nov. 23, 1993

To acknowledge the 100th anniversary of the January 17, 1893 overthrow of the Kingdom of Hawaii, and to offer an apology to Native Hawaiians on behalf of the United States for the overthrow of the Kingdom of Hawaii.

Whereas, prior to the arrival of the first Europeans in 1778, the Native Hawaiian people lived in a highly organized, self-sufficient, subsistent social system based on communal land tenure with a sophisticated language, culture, and religion;

Whereas, a unified monarchical government of the Hawaiian Islands was established in 1810 under Kamehameha I, the first King of Hawaii;

Whereas, from 1826 until 1893, the United States recognized the independence of the Kingdom of Hawaii, extended full and complete diplomatic recognition to the Hawaiian Government, and entered into treaties and conventions with the Hawaiian monarchs to govern commerce and navigation in 1826, 1842, 1849, 1875, and 1887;

Whereas, the Congregational Church (now known as the United Church of Christ), through its American Board of

Commissioners for Foreign Missions, sponsored and sent more than 100 missionaries to the Kingdom of Hawaii between 1820 and 1850;

Whereas, on January 14, 1893, John L. Stevens (hereafter referred to in this Resolution as the "United States Minister"), the United States Minister assigned to the sovereign and independent Kingdom of Hawaii conspired with a small group of non-Hawaiian residents of the Kingdom of Hawaii, including citizens of the United States, to overthrow the indigenous and lawful Government of Hawaii;

Whereas, in pursuance of the conspiracy to overthrow the Government of Hawaii, the United States Minister and the naval representatives of the United States caused armed naval forces of the United States to invade the sovereign Hawaiian nation on January 16, 1893, and to position themselves near the Hawaiian Government buildings and the Iolani Palace to intimidate Queen Liliuokalani and her Government;

Whereas, on the afternoon of January 17,1893, a Committee of Safety that represented the American and European sugar planters, descendants of missionaries, and financiers deposed the Hawaiian monarchy and proclaimed the establishment of a Provisional Government;

Whereas, the United States Minister thereupon extended diplomatic recognition to the Provisional Government that was formed by the conspirators without the consent of the Native Hawaiian people or the lawful Government of Hawaii and in violation of treaties between the two nations and of international law;

Whereas, soon thereafter, when informed of the risk of bloodshed with resistance, Queen Liliuokalani issued the following statement yielding her authority to the United States Government rather than to the provisional government:

"I Liliuokalani, by the Grace of God and under the Constitution of the Hawaiian Kingdom, Queen, do hereby solemnly protest against any and all acts done against myself and the Constitutional Government of the Hawaiian Kingdom by certain persons claiming to have established a Provisional Government of and for this Kingdom."

"That I yield to the superior force of the United States of America whose Minister Plenipotentiary, His Excellency John L. Stevens, has caused United States troops to be landed at Honolulu and declared that he would support the provisional government."

"Now to avoid any collision of armed forces, and perhaps the loss of life, I do this under protest and impelled by said force yield my authority until such time as the Government of the United States shall, upon facts being presented to it, undo the action of its representatives and reinstate me in the authority which I claim as the Constitutional Sovereign of the Hawaiian Islands."

Done at Honolulu this 17th day of January, A.D. 1893.;

Whereas, without the active support and intervention by the United States diplomatic and military representatives, the insurrection against the Government of Queen Liliuokalani would have failed for lack of popular support and insufficient arms;

Whereas, on February 1, 1893, the United States Minister raised the American flag and proclaimed Hawaii to be a protectorate of the United States;

Whereas, the report of a presidentially-established investigation conducted by former Congressman James Blount into the events surrounding the insurrection and overthrow of January 17, 1893, concluded that the United States diplomatic and military representatives had abused their authority and were responsible for the change in government;

Whereas, as a result of this investigation, the United States Minister to Hawaii was recalled from his diplomatic post and the military commander of the United States armed forces stationed in Hawaii was disciplined and forced to resign his commission;

Whereas, in a message to Congress on December 18, 1893, President Grover Cleveland reported fully and accurately on the illegal acts of the conspirators, described such acts as an "act of war, committed with the participation of a diplomatic representative of the United States and without authority of Congress", and acknowledged that by such acts the government of a peaceful and friendly people was overthrown;

Whereas, President Cleveland further concluded that a "substantial wrong has thus been done which a due regard for our national character as well as the rights of the injured people requires we should endeavor to repair" and called for the restoration of the Hawaiian monarchy;

Whereas, the Provisional Government protested President Cleveland's call for the restoration of the monarchy and continued to hold state power and pursue annexation to the United States;

Whereas, the Provisional Government successfully lobbied the Committee on Foreign Relations of the Senate (hereafter referred to in this Resolution as the "Committee") to conduct a new investigation into the events surrounding the overthrow of the monarchy;

Whereas, the Committee and its chairman, Senator John Morgan, conducted hearings in Washington, D.C., from December 27,1893, through February 26, 1894, in which members of the Provisional Government justified and condoned the actions of the United States Minister and recommended annexation of Hawaii;

Whereas, although the Provisional Government was able to obscure the role of the United States in the illegal overthrow of the Hawaiian monarchy, it was unable to rally the support from two-thirds of the Senate needed to ratify a treaty of annexation;

Whereas, on July 4, 1894, the Provisional Government declared itself to be the Republic of Hawaii;

Whereas, on January 24, 1895, while imprisoned in Iolani Palace, Queen Liliuokalani was forced by representatives of the Republic of Hawaii to officially abdicate her throne;

Whereas, in the 1896 United States Presidential election, William McKinley replaced Grover Cleveland;

Whereas, on July 7, 1898, as a consequence of the Spanish-American War, President McKinley signed the Newlands Joint Resolution that provided for the annexation of Hawaii;

Whereas, through the Newlands Resolution, the self-declared Republic of Hawaii ceded sovereignty over the Hawaiian Islands to the United States;

Whereas, the Republic of Hawaii also ceded 1,800,000 acres of crown, government and public lands of the Kingdom of

Hawaii, without the consent of or compensation to the Native Hawaiian people of Hawaii or their sovereign government;

Whereas, the Congress, through the Newlands Resolution, ratified the cession, annexed Hawaii as part of the United States, and vested title to the lands in Hawaii in the United States;

Whereas, the Newlands Resolution also specified that treaties existing between Hawaii and foreign nations were to immediately cease and be replaced by United States treaties with such nations;

Whereas, the Newlands Resolution effected the transaction between the Republic of Hawaii and the United States Government;

Whereas, **the indigenous Hawaiian people never directly relinquished their claims to their inherent sovereignty as a people or over their national lands to the United States, either through their monarchy or through a plebiscite or referendum**; (emphasis added)

Whereas, on April 30, 1900, President McKinley signed the Organic Act that provided a government for the territory of

Hawaii and defined the political structure and powers of the newly established Territorial Government and its relationship to the United States;

Whereas, on August 21,1959, Hawaii became the 50th State of the United States;

Whereas, the health and well-being of the Native Hawaiian people is intrinsically tied to their deep feelings and attachment to the land;

Whereas, the long-range economic and social changes in Hawaii over the nineteenth and early twentieth centuries have been devastating to the population and to the health and well-being of the Hawaiian people;

Whereas, the Native Hawaiian people are determined to preserve, develop and transmit to future generations their ancestral territory, and their cultural identity in accordance with their own spiritual and traditional beliefs, customs, practices, language, and social institutions;

Whereas, in order to promote racial harmony and cultural understanding, the Legislature of the State of Hawaii has determined that the year 1993, should serve Hawaii as a year of special reflection on the rights and dignities of the Native Hawaiians in the Hawaiian and the American societies;

Whereas, the Eighteenth General Synod of the United Church of Christ in recognition of the denomination's historical complicity in the illegal overthrow of the Kingdom of Hawaii in 1893 directed the Office of the President of the United Church of Christ to offer a public apology to the Native Hawaiian people and to initiate the process of reconciliation between the United Church of Christ and the Native Hawaiians; and

Whereas, it is proper and timely for the Congress on the occasion of the impending one hundredth anniversary of the event, to acknowledge the historic significance of the illegal overthrow of the Kingdom of Hawaii, to express its deep regret to the Native Hawaiian people, and to support the reconciliation efforts of the State of Hawaii and the United Church of Christ with Native Hawaiians;

Now, therefore, be it

Resolved by the Senate and House of Representatives of the United States of America in Congress assembled,

SECTION 1. ACKNOWLEDGMENT AND APOLOGY.

The Congress -

(1) on the occasion of the 100th anniversary of the illegal overthrow of the Kingdom of Hawaii on January 17, 1893, acknowledges the historical significance of this event which resulted in the suppression of the inherent sovereignty of the Native Hawaiian people;

(2) recognizes and commends efforts of reconciliation initiated by the State of Hawaii and the United Church of Christ with Native Hawaiians;

(3) apologizes to Native Hawaiians on behalf of the people of the United States for the overthrow of the Kingdom of Hawaii on January 17, 1893 with the participation of agents and citizens of the United States, and the deprivation of the rights of Native Hawaiians to self-determination;

(4) expresses its commitment to acknowledge the ramifications of the overthrow of the Kingdom of Hawaii, in

order to provide a proper foundation for reconciliation between the United States and the Native Hawaiian people; and

(5) urges the President of the United States to also acknowledge the ramifications of the overthrow of the Kingdom of Hawaii and to support reconciliation efforts between the United States and the Native Hawaiian people.

SEC. 2. DEFINITIONS.

As used in this Joint Resolution, the term "Native Hawaiians" means any individual who is a descendent of the aboriginal people who, prior to 1778, occupied and exercised sovereignty in the area that now constitutes the State of Hawaii.

SEC. 3. DISCLAIMER.

Nothing in this Joint Resolution is intended to serve as a settlement of any claims against the United States.

Approved November 23, 1993

Rev. James D. Kimmel

LEGISLATIVE HISTORY - S.J. Res. 19:

SENATE REPORTS: No. 103-125 (Select Comm. on Indian Affairs)

CONGRESSIONAL RECORD, Vol. 139 (1993).

Public Law 103-150 opened the door to the possibility of world peace because it presents the foundation for truth and justice for Hawai'i, a Nation occupied by the U. S. government for over one hundred years. Truth and justice for Hawai'i means truth and justice for America, and that means a bust for Uncle Sam and the United States Government. In the course of the political evolution of the United States going from 13 to 50 States, a long train of abuses and usurpations were consummated in violation of international public law, The Law of Nations, and the Constitution of the United States.

Included here is a copy of Queen Liliuokalani's **Official Protest** to the U. S. plan to Annex Hawai'i as a Territory of the United States, and I draw your attention to the bottom line: ***...and to the Almighty Ruler of the Universe, to Him who judgeth righteously, I commit my cause.***

MY OFFICIAL PROTEST TO THE TREATY

"I, LILIUOKALANI of Hawai'i, by the will of God named heir apparent on the tenth day of April, A.D. 1877, and by the grace of God Queen of the Hawaiian Islands on the seventeenth day of January, A.D. 1893, do hereby protest against the ratification of a certain treaty, which, so I am informed, has been signed at Washington by Messrs. Hatch, Thurston, and Kinney, purporting to cede those Islands to the territory and dominion of the United States. I declare such a treaty to be an act of wrong toward the native and part-native people of Hawai'i, an invasion of the rights of the ruling chiefs, in violation of international rights both toward my people and toward friendly nations with whom they have made treaties, the perpetuation of the fraud whereby the constitutional government was overthrown, and, finally, an act of gross injustice to me."

"Because the official protests made by me on the seventeenth day of January, 1893, to the so-called provisional Government was signed by me, and received by said government with the assurance that the case was referred to the United States of America for arbitration."

YIELDED TO AVOID BLOODSHED.

"Because that protest and my communications to the United States Government immediately thereafter expressly declare that I yielded my authority to the forces of the United States in order to avoid bloodshed, and because I recognized the futility of a conflict with so formidable a power."

"Because the President of the United States, the Secretary of State, and an envoy commissioned by them reported in official documents that my government was unlawfully coerced by the forces, diplomatic and naval, of the United States; that I was at the date of their investigations the constitutional ruler of my people."

"Because such decision of the recognized magistrates of the United States was officially communicated to me and to Sanford B. Dole, and said Dole's resignation requested by Albert S. Willis, the recognized agent and minister of the Government of the United States."

"Because neither the above-named commission nor the government which sends it has ever received any such authority from the registered voters of Hawai'i, but derives its assumed powers from the so-called committee of public safety, organized on or about the seventeenth day of January, 1893, said committee being composed largely of persons claiming American citizenship, and not one single Hawaiian was a member thereof, or in any way participated in the demonstration leading to its existence."

"Because my people, about forty thousand in number, have in no way been consulted by those, three thousand in number, who claim the right to destroy the independence of Hawaii. My people constitute four-fifths of the legally qualified voters of Hawaii, and excluding those imported for the demands of labor, about the same proportion of the inhabitants."

CIVIC AND HEREDITARY RIGHTS.

"Because said treaty ignores, not only the civic rights of my people, but, further, the hereditary property of their chiefs. Of the 4,000,000 acres composing the territory said treaty offers to annex, 1,000,000 or 915,000 acres has in no way been heretofore recognized as other than the private property of the constitutional monarch, subject to a control in no way differing from other items of a private estate."

"Because it is proposed by said treaty to confiscate said property, technically called the crown lands, those legally entitled thereto, either now or in succession, receiving no consideration whatever for estates, their title to which has been always undisputed, and which is legitimately in my name at this date."

"Because said treaty ignores, not only all professions of perpetual amity and good faith made by the United States in former treaties with the sovereigns representing the Hawaiian people, but all treaties made by those sovereigns with other and friendly powers, and it is thereby in violation of international law."

"Because, by treating with the parties claiming at this time the right to cede said territory of Hawaii, the Government of the United States receives such territory from the hands of those whom its own magistrates (legally elected by the people of the United States, and in office in 1893) pronounced fraudulently in power and unconstitutionally ruling Hawaii."

APPEALS TO PRESIDENT AND SENATE.

"Therefore I, Liliuokalani of Hawaii, do hereby call upon the President of that nation, to whom alone I yielded my property and my authority, to withdraw said treaty (ceding said Islands) from further consideration. I ask the honorable Senate of the United States to decline to ratify said treaty, and I implore the people of this great and good nation, from whom my ancestors learned the Christian religion, to sustain their representatives in such acts of justice and equity as may be in accord with the principles of their fathers, and to the Almighty Ruler of the universe, to him who judgeth righteously, I commit my cause."

"Done at Washington, District of Columbia, United States of America, this seventeenth day of June, in the year eighteen hundred and ninety-seven."

"Liliuokalani."

"Joseph Heleluhe, }"

"Wokeki Heleluhe, } Witnesses to Signature."

"Julius A. Palmer. }"

So now, God wants the world to know the truth about Himself, Hawai'I, and Jesus, as well as Lucifer, Satan, and the Devil, all of whom have been grossly misrepresented to the people of this world. For truth and justice to reign in Hawai'i and for peace to reign on earth, a major, **Epochal Revelation** was required and **THE URANTIA BOOK** was brought into existence in 1934-1935, the very years of my conception and birth!

This book fills in all the missing links in our chain of understanding how things have come to be the way they are on earth and in the Universe. To me, it is the Cosmology of the Unified Field of an Infinite Universe of Eternal existence. Without this revelation at this time in our evolutionary development, I don't think we'd make it to group survival before we'd make it to group extinction. This book provides the power of knowledge and the reality of truth essential to the liberation of the people of the United States and the world. If it is not a good example of divine intervention in our local and global affairs, I don't know what is.

But it is like *Cannabis*, marijuana, in that you have to read it and experience it within yourself to know the truth about it. And you can't know the truth about God, *The Urantia Book,* or marijuana without first-hand personal experience, for which there is no cosmic substitute unless you trust another person who knows the truth and shares it with you.

The Road Map to World Peace includes *The Urantia Book,* which reveals *the Pathway of Infinite Perfection* (p 1965) that leads there because one must become truth-coordinated to get on this Route to World Peace, all the way to Paradise and the Geographic Center of Infinity where the Eternal Gods have always resided. Part II of this book reveals that the person the Queen of Hawai'i appealed to in her Official Protest is none other than the Sovereign Ruler and Creator Father of the Universe we all live in. Part IV of this book reveals the Life and Teachings of Jesus, who is our older human brother, the Sovereign Creator of the Universe incarnate in human form, doing what he must do to retrieve our planet from rebellion and reinstate the rule of the government and the Law of our Universe on earth.

On page 1948 of *The Urantia Book*, Jesus tells his apostles about **The Promised Helper, the Spirit of Truth**, saying: "When I have gone to the Father, and after he has fully accepted the work I have done for you on earth, and after I have received the final sovereignty of my own domain, I shall say to my Father: Having left my children alone on earth, it is in accordance with my promise to send them another teacher. And when the Father shall approve, I will pour out the Spirit of Truth upon all flesh. Already is my Father's spirit in your hearts, and when this day shall come, you will also have me with you even as you now have the Father. This new gift is the spirit of living truth. The unbelievers will not at first listen to the teachings of this spirit, but the sons of light will all receive him gladly and with a whole heart. And you shall know this spirit when he comes even as you have known me, and you will receive this gift in your hearts, and he will abide with you. You thus perceive that I am not going to leave you without help and guidance. I will not leave you desolate. Today I can be with you only in person. In the times to come I will be with you and all other men who desire my presence, wherever you may be, and with each of you at the same time. Do you not discern that it is better for me to go away; that I leave you in the flesh so that I may the better and the more fully be with you in the spirit?"

"In just a few hours the world will see me no more; but you will continue to know me in your hearts even until I send you this new teacher, the Spirit of Truth. As I have lived with you in person, then shall I live in you; I shall be one with your personal experience in the spirit kingdom. And when this has come to pass, you shall surely know that I am in the Father, and that, while your life is hid with the Father in me, I am also in you. I have loved the Father and have kept his word; you have loved me, and you will keep my word. As my Father has given me of his spirit, so will I give you of my spirit. And this Spirit of Truth which I will bestow upon you shall guide and comfort you and shall eventually lead you into all truth."

"I am telling you these things while I am still with you that you may be the better prepared to endure those trials which are even now right upon us. And when this new day comes, you will be indwelt by the Son as well as by the Father. And these gifts of heaven will ever work the one with the other even as the Father and I have wrought on earth and before your very eyes as one person, the Son of Man. And this spirit friend will bring to your remembrance everything I have taught you."

"As the Master paused for a moment, Judas Alpheus made bold to ask one of the few questions which either he or his brother ever addressed to Jesus in public. Said Judas: Master, you have always lived among us as a friend; how shall we know you when you no longer manifest yourself to us save by this spirit? If the world sees you not, how shall we be certain about you? How will you show yourself to us?"

"Jesus looked down upon them all, smiled, and said: My little children, I am going away, going back to my Father. In a little while you will not see me as you do here, as flesh and blood. In a very short time I am going to send you my spirit, just like me except for this material body. This new teacher is the Spirit of Truth who will live with each one of you, in your hearts, and so will all the children of light be made one and be drawn toward one another. And in this very manner will my Father and I be able to live in the souls of each one of you and also in the hearts of all other men who love us and make that love real in their experiences by loving one another, even as I am now loving you."

"Judas Alpheus did not fully understand what the Master said, but he grasped the promise of the new teacher, and from the expression on Andrew's face, he perceived that his question had been satisfactorily answered."

"The new helper which Jesus promised to send into the hearts of believers, to pour out upon all flesh, is the Spirit of Truth. This divine endowment is not the letter or law of truth, neither is it to function as the form or expression of truth. The new teacher is the *conviction* of truth, the consciousness and assurance of true meanings on real spirit levels. And this new teacher is the spirit of living and growing truth, expanding, unfolding, and adaptative truth."

"Divine truth is a spirit-discerned and living reality. Truth exists only on high spiritual levels of the realization of divinity and the consciousness of communion with God. You can know the truth, and you can live the truth; you can experience the growth of truth in the soul and enjoy the liberty of its enlightenment in the mind, but you cannot imprison truth in formulas, codes, creeds, or intellectual patterns of human conduct. When you undertake the human formulation of divine truth, it speedily dies. The post-mortem salvage of imprisoned truth, even at best, can eventuate only in the realization of a peculiar form of intellectualized glorified wisdom. Static truth is dead truth, and only dead truth can be held as a theory. Living truth is dynamic and can enjoy only an experiential existence in the human mind."

"Intelligence grows out of a material existence which is illuminated by the presence of the cosmic mind. Wisdom comprises the consciousness of knowledge elevated to new levels of meaning and activated by the presence of the universe endowment of the adjutant of wisdom. Truth is a spiritual reality value experienced only by spirit-endowed beings who function upon super-material levels of universe consciousness, and who, after the realization of truth, permit its spirit of activation to live and reign within their souls."

"The true child of universe insight looks for the living Spirit of Truth in every wise saying. The God-knowing individual is constantly elevating wisdom to the living-truth levels of divine attainment; the spiritually unprogressive soul is all the while dragging the living truth down to the dead levels of wisdom and to the domain of mere exalted knowledge."

"The golden rule, when divested of the superhuman insight of the Spirit of Truth, becomes nothing more than a rule of high ethical conduct. The golden rule, when literally interpreted, may become the instrument of great offense to one's fellows. Without a spiritual discernment of the golden rule of wisdom you might reason that, since you are desirous that all men speak the full and frank truth of their minds to you, you should therefore fully and frankly speak the full thought of your mind to your fellow beings. Such an unspiritual interpretation of the golden rule might result in untold unhappiness and no end of sorrow."

"Some persons discern and interpret the golden rule as a purely intellectual affirmation of human fraternity. Others experience this expression of human relationship as an emotional gratification of the tender feelings of the human personality. Another mortal recognizes this same golden rule as the yardstick for measuring all social relations, the standard of social conduct. Still others look upon it as being the positive injunction of a great moral teacher who embodied in this statement the highest concept of moral obligation as regards all fraternal relationships. In the lives of such moral beings the golden rule becomes the wise center and circumference of all their philosophy."

"In the kingdom of the believing brotherhood of God-knowing truth lovers, this golden rule takes on living qualities of spiritual realization on those higher levels of interpretation which cause the mortal sons of God to view this injunction of the Master as requiring them so to relate themselves to their fellows that they will receive the highest possible good as a result of the believer's contact with them. This is the essence of true religion: that you love your neighbor as yourself."

"But the highest realization and the truest interpretation of the golden rule consists in the consciousness of the spirit of the truth of the enduring and living reality of such a divine declaration. The true cosmic meaning of this rule of universal relationship is revealed only in its spiritual realization, in the interpretation of the law of conduct by the spirit of the Son to the spirit of the Father that indwells the soul of mortal man. And when such spirit-led mortals realize the true meaning of this golden rule, they are filled to overflowing with the assurance of citizenship in a friendly universe, and their ideals of spirit reality are satisfied only when they love their fellows as Jesus loved us all, and that is the reality of the realization of the love of God."

"This same philosophy of the living flexibility and cosmic adaptability of divine truth to the individual requirements and capacity of every son of God, must be perceived before you can hope adequately to understand the Master's teaching and practice of nonresistance to evil. The Master's teaching is basically a spiritual pronouncement. Even the material implications of his philosophy cannot be helpfully considered apart from their spiritual correlations. The spirit of the Master's injunction consists in the nonresistance of all selfish reaction to the universe, coupled with the aggressive and progressive attainment of righteous levels of true spirit values: divine beauty, infinite goodness, and eternal truth — to know God and to become increasingly like him."

"Love, unselfishness, must undergo a constant and living readaptative interpretation of relationships in accordance with the leading of the Spirit of Truth. Love must thereby grasp the ever-changing and enlarging concepts of the highest cosmic good of the individual who is loved. And then love goes on to strike this same attitude concerning all other individuals who could possibly be influenced by the growing and living relationship of one spirit-led mortal's love for other citizens of the universe. And this entire living adaptation of love must be effected in the light of both the environment of present evil and the eternal goal of the perfection of divine destiny."

"And so must we clearly recognize that neither the golden rule nor the teaching of nonresistance can ever be properly understood as dogmas or precepts. They can only be comprehended by living them, by realizing their meanings in the living interpretation of the Spirit of Truth, who directs the loving contact of one human being with another."

"And all this clearly indicates the difference between the old religion and the new. The old religion taught self-sacrifice; the new religion teaches only self-forgetfulness, enhanced self-realization in conjoined social service and universe comprehension. The old religion was motivated by fear-consciousness; the new gospel of the kingdom is dominated by truth-conviction, the spirit of eternal and universal truth. And no amount of piety or creedal loyalty can compensate for the absence in the life experience of kingdom believers of that spontaneous, generous, and sincere friendliness which characterizes the spirit-born sons of the living God. Neither tradition nor a ceremonial system of formal worship can atone for the lack of genuine compassion for one's fellows."

The world is now face to face-to-face with the most powerful military government and the most dangerous sovereignty-wielding-president in the history of the United States. The history of the evolution of the fifty United States of America discloses a long train of abuses of power and usurpations of rights. The consequences of so many betrayals of trust and abrogations of the Supreme Law of the Land are nothing less than the overthrow of the United States Government. You cannot do to others as you would not have them do unto you without experiencing exactly what you are dishing out. The overthrow of so many governments and occupation of so many other nations by the U. S. government has resulted in the overthrow of the U. S. government simply because of the failure of politicians and the general public to live in harmony with the will of God and the Supreme Law of the Land.

Democracy is an ideal. It is a product of civilization, not of evolution. From this point on, we should go more slowly and select more carefully because of the dangers of democracy, which are:

1. Glorification of mediocrity.

2. Choice of base and ignorant rulers.

3. Failure to recognize the basic facts of social evolution.

4. Danger of universal suffrage in the hands of uneducated and indolent majorities.

5. Slavery to public opinion; the majority is not always right.

On page 802 of *The Urantia Book*, it says: "Public opinion, common opinion, has always delayed society; nevertheless, it is valuable, for, while retarding social evolution, it does preserve civilization. Education of public opinion is the only safe and true method of accelerating civilization; force is only a temporary expedient, and cultural growth will increasingly accelerate as bullets give way to ballots. Public opinion, the mores, is the basic and elemental energy in social evolution and state development, but to be of state value it must be nonviolent in expression."

"The measure of the advance of society is directly determined by the degree to which public opinion can control personal behavior and state regulation through nonviolent expression. The really civilized government had arrived when public opinion was clothed with the powers of personal franchise. Popular elections may not always decide things rightly, but they represent the right way even to do a wrong thing. Evolution does not at once produce superlative perfection but rather comparative and advancing practical adjustment."

Representative government presupposes an intelligent, efficient, and universal electorate. But the majority of the American Electorate has been blinded and made crazy without their realizing it by trusting and believing their political and religious leaders who have been misleading and misfeeding them with a long train of false facts and untruths for so many years that treason, war, and mass murder have become socially acceptable.

In the case of Henry Noa, the Prime Minister of the reinstated, Lawful Hawaiian Government versus Linda Lingle and the State of Hawai'i and George W. Bush and the United States of America, the de facto governments presently overcontrolling the people and natural resources of Hawai'i, it is highly questionable as to whether they will voluntarily submit themselves and their governments to the Rule of International, Constitutional, and Universal Law in harmony with the will of God, or not!

I pray for the righteous adjudication of the case of Liliuokalani, Queen of Hawai'i, versus the United States Government for the equal benefit of the people of Hawai'i, America, and the world. Truth and justice for Hawai'i and the United States means the eventual reinstatement of both the lawful Hawaiian and the lawful American Governments that have long been overthrown. I pray for a successful transition period during which time the State of Hawai'i and the United States Government return their authority and responsibility for Hawai'i to the reinstated Hawaiian Government, the Kingdom of Hawai'i, and humbly remove themselves from the Hawaiian Archipelago and the Nation of Hawai'i. I pray for the recognition of the reinstated Hawaiian Government by other nations relative to the implementation of peace on earth and good will among all men. I pray that the reinstated Hawaiian Government will extend invitations to the heads of state and the foreign ministers of every nation on earth for a Global Constitutional Convention, to be held in Hawai'i and hosted by the lawful Hawaiian Government. And lastly, I pray that Hawai'i becomes the capitol of a New Form of representative World Government of all humankind, by all humankind, and for all humankind and all nations, in harmony with and coordinate with the functioning of the reinstated Hawaiian Government.

So if we follow the Pathway of Infinite Perfection, the Great Highway of the Golden Rule, and The Law of Nations, this Road Map will take you and yours toward heaven on earth and good will among all men. And we can have it if we want it because of the fact that you get what you choose, not what you don't choose. However, in all these things, it is my will that the will of God be done: in my life, your life, and the lives of all of our brothers and sisters in the brotherhood of all humankind.

P. S. I look forward to the festivities of Peace Week in the future and the Grand Celebration of our world's first Planetary Holiday, *Global Independence Day,* on August 21, 20??, in commemoration of the birthday of Jesus of Nazareth, our older human brother as well as the incarnate Creator and Sovereign Ruler of our Local Universe.

About the Author

The author and father of five children was born on March 2, 1935 and raised on his family's dairy farm near Canton, Ohio. He graduated from Canton McKinley high school in 1953 and was first married in Honolulu, Hawai'i in February, 1957. He then graduated from The Ohio State University with the degrees B.Sc. in 1958 and M.Sc. in 1960. He spent **ten years on the ecological and nuclear frontiers** from Ohio State to the Marshall Islands and the Nevada Test Sites from 1962-1967. Kimmel was divorced in 1967 and began teaching high school the same year in Novato, California. He was arrested for Cannabis (marijuana) possession in 1968 and completed Dr. Einstein's unfinished Unified Field Theory, deriving **the Unified Field Equation, *1* = ∞**, in February, 1969. After recognizing the fact of God, he discovered *THE URANTIA BOOK* as the greatest thing to hit the planet since Jesus, opening *The Religion of Jesus Church* near Sonoma, California in October, 1969, *The Religion of Jesus Church Divinity School* in Kekaha, Kauai in 1973, and *The Religion of Jesus Farm* on Molokai from 1974-78. He entered the political frontier of the Hawaiian Sovereignty Movement in 1973 and was on the ballot against Senator Dan Inouye in 1974. Kimmel spent 26 months incarcerated at the Federal Corrections Institute at Terminal

Island, California before having his convictions reversed on Appeal to the Ninth Circuit Court in 1982. In 1985 he founded an instrumentality for world peace, a non-profit public benefit corporation known as *Peace, Incorporated*, whose web site is located at: **www.maui.net/~peaceinc.** The author became a Citizen-Applicant of the lawful (de jure) **Reinstated Hawaiian Government** in 1999 and continues to work toward World Peace and a **Global Constitutional Convention** for the purpose of creating a *Master Charter of Liberty*, a **Constitution of World Law, for the implementation of a New Form of World Government of the People, by the People and for the People and the Nations of the World, requisite to the actualization and establishment of World Peace.**